A NOTE TO PARENTS

When your children are ready to "step into reading," giving them the right books—and lots of them—is as crucial as giving them the right food to eat. **Step into Reading Books** present exciting stories and information reinforced with lively, colorful illustrations that make learning to read fun, satisfying, and worthwhile. They are priced so that acquiring an entire library of them is affordable. And they are beginning readers with an important difference—they're written on four levels.

Step 1 Books, with their very large type and extremely simple vocabulary, have been created for the very youngest readers. **Step 2 Books** are both longer and slightly more difficult. **Step 3 Books,** written to mid-second-grade reading levels, are for the child who has acquired even greater reading skills. **Step 4 Books** offer exciting nonfiction for the increasingly proficient reader.

Children develop at different ages. **Step into Reading Books,** with their four levels of reading, are designed to help children become good—and interested—readers *faster*. The grade levels assigned to the four steps—preschool through grade 1 for Step 1, grades 1 through 3 for Step 2, grades 2 and 3 for Step 3, and grades 2 through 4 for Step 4—are intended only as guides. Some children move through all four steps very rapidly; others climb the steps over a period of several years. These books will help your child "step into reading" in style!

For Emily and Orson

Library of Congress Cataloging-in-Publication Data: Buller, Jon, 1943– . Space rock. (Step into reading.
A Step 3 book) SUMMARY: Bob helps a talking rock return to the planet Kal-dor. [1. Rocks—Fiction.
2. Extraterrestrial beings—Fiction] I. Schade, Susan. II. Title. III. Series: Step into Reading. Step
3 book. PZ7.B9135Sp 1988 [E] 87-12762 ISBN: 0-394-89384-0 (pbk.); 0-394-99384-5 (lib. bdg.)

Manufactured in the United States of America   8 9 0

STEP INTO READING is a trademark of Random House, Inc.

Step into Reading

SPACE ROCK

By Jon Buller
and Susan Schade

A Step 3 Book

Random House 🏠 New York

My name is Bob. I go to Center School. I am going to tell you a strange story. You may not believe it. But it is true.

It all started on the day of our big class project. We were standing in the schoolyard. Miss Goodheart was blowing up my balloon.

Soon every kid had a balloon. And every balloon had a little post card tied to it.

Wherever the balloons landed, people would find the cards and mail them back to us.

I held on tight to my red balloon.

"Ready, class?" called Miss Goodheart.

We all let go at once. Up, up, and away went the balloons.

"Hey, look!" someone shouted. "There's one caught in a tree!"

"It's probably Bob's," someone else said. "Ha, ha, ha!"

It <u>was</u> a red one. It probably was mine. I was that kind of kid.

Then a gust of wind pulled it loose.
The red balloon sailed into a cloud and
disappeared.

"All right!" I said. I punched the air.

After school I walked home by myself. I was humming and kicking a can. Where had my balloon gone? Who knows. Maybe it was on its way to Mars!

The can rolled under a bush. I reached in and felt around. I couldn't find it.

Instead I pulled out a rock.
It was sort of shiny, as if it had glitter on it. And it looked like it had a face. It was neat.
I put it in my pocket and went home.

When I got home, I put the rock on my
desk. Then I did my math homework. Math
is always hard for me.

"Now, what is thirty-seven plus fourteen?"
I thought to myself. I held the rock and
turned it over in my hands.

"Fifty-one!" It was almost like I heard a
voice. The answer just popped into my head.

Wow! That was easy. That night I got
my homework done in no time.

After dinner I played with my race
cars. I put the rock in one car and a big
marble in the other car.

The rock won every race.

Maybe I was crazy. But the rock almost
looked like it was smiling!

That night I put the rock on my table.
It seemed to be glowing. I got into bed.

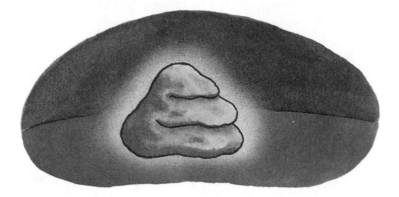

Then I heard a little noise. It
sounded like a lawn mower far away. Or
like a bee buzzing. Where was the noise
coming from? I wasn't sure.

I got back in bed and turned out the light. Once again I heard the noise. Now I was sure the noise was in my room. And it seemed to come from the glowing rock!

I picked up the rock. I held it next to my ear.

"CAN YOU HEAR ME NOW, BOB?"

I almost fell out of bed!

"TIME IS RUNNING OUT!" shouted the rock. "I NEED YOUR HELP!"

"Wow!" I said. "I never saw a talking rock before. And you don't need to shout. I can hear you now."

"Good," said the rock. "That shouting was using up all my energy. You humans don't hear very well, do you?"

This is what the rock told me.

"I come from the planet Kal-dor," he began. "My planet is big and flat. There are no hills, no trees, no rivers. There are no roads, no houses, no race cars. We just float above the ground and take energy from the sun."

"Gee, it sounds like a fun place," I said.

"Very funny," said the rock. "It's my home and I like it. But I wanted to explore the galaxy. I wanted to go farther than any rock has ever gone.

"So some friends and I got a spaceship. We blasted off. After many years we came to your planet."

"We call it earth," I said.

"I know," the rock said. "It is a very nice planet. It is one of the nicest planets I have ever seen."

"Thank you," I said.

"We flew over mountains and seas and deserts and cities. It has been very interesting for us. We took pictures to show the other rocks at home. We traveled only at night."

"Why?" I asked.

"So that no one would see us," said the rock.

"Why didn't you want anyone to see you?" I asked.

"It is safer," he said.

"Why?" I said.

The rock sounded mad. "Because humans are too nosy. They ask too many questions!"

"Oh," I said.

The rock went on with his story.

"Then today a terrible thing happened. We were hiding in a cloud over your town. We saw a lot of little humans in a field. Then a lot of round things with tails floated up in the air."

"That was us!" I cried, jumping on the bed. "The whole class sent off post cards on balloons!"

The rock looked amazed. "Balloons! We
thought they were lost creatures from
another planet! So we opened the ship and
one floated in. Then there was a big bang
and it was gone. We all jumped back in
surprise. That's when I fell out of the ship!

"I found that I could not float in the air around earth. Down, down I went. I landed under a bush.

"It was dark under the bush. The sun didn't shine on me. My friends couldn't see me. What if they return to Kal-dor without me?" he cried. "I am doomed!"

"Don't worry," I said. "It will be all right. I'll carry you around. Together we will find your ship!"

I put the rock on my pillow. "I will call you Space Rock," I said.

It took me a long time to fall asleep that night. I was so excited! Nothing ever happened to me. And now I had a rock from outer space. Wait until the other kids saw this!

The next day I got up early. I put Space Rock into my lunch box.

"Don't eat all my food," I said jokingly.

"Eating is for humans," said Space Rock. "Just give me a few juicy rays of sun."

When we got to school I put Space Rock on my desk. I put him in a nice sunny spot.

First period was science. We looked at mushrooms and bugs under a magnifying glass.

Then Miss Goodheart said, "Does anyone have anything for show and tell?"

I waved my hand.

"I do! I do, Miss Goodheart!" I said.

"All right, Bob," she said.

"This is Space Rock," I said to the class. "He looks just like any rock. But he is really from another planet! Yesterday one of our balloons popped inside his spaceship and he fell out!"

"Ha ha ha ha ha ha ha ha ha ha ha ha ha ha ha ha ha ha ha ha ha ha ha ha ha ha ha ha!" said the class.

"That's a good story, Bob," said Miss
Goodheart. "Did you make it up yourself?"

"No," I said. "I did not make it up.
It is true.

"Hold him up to your ear. He will
talk to you," I said.

"This better not be a trick," said
Miss Goodheart. She held Space Rock next
to her ear.

The kids in the class were falling out
of their chairs laughing.

"Well," said Miss Goodheart, "maybe
your hearing is better than mine."

She gave Space Rock back to me.

She did not believe me.

After show and tell we went outside for recess.

I took Space Rock out of my pocket. "Why didn't you talk to Miss Goodheart?" I demanded.

"You shouldn't have told them who I was!" he hissed back at me. "If Miss Goodheart believed you, she would have called the police! Or the President! They would lock me up in a glass case in a museum next to a piece of the moon! They would ask me questions!"

"Did you see everyone laughing at me?" I said. "You made me look like a fool!"

Both of us were mad.

Some of the kids started laughing again. "Talking to Space Rock, Bob?" they asked.

I stuck Space Rock into my pocket. Then all at once Space Rock felt very warm. "Bob!" he cried from inside my pocket. "Bob, it's my ship! I can feel them nearby! Put me in the sun!"

I held him up in the sunlight. He was really shining now.

"It's no good, Bob!" he cried. "I feel them going again. They still don't see me. I'm not shining enough."

"Wait! I have an idea," I told Space Rock. I ran back into the schoolroom. I found Miss Goodheart's magnifying glass. I took it outside.

I held the magnifying glass over Space Rock. Everybody was watching. Now a beam of light bounced off Space Rock back up into the sky.

"I bet your spaceship will find you now!" I said.

The kids' eyes opened wide.

"We'd better get the nurse. Bob is in really bad shape," I heard someone say.

But then the kids jumped back and their eyes opened even wider.

They pointed over my head.

Space Rock's ship was coming down!

The spaceship came closer and closer. It hung in the air right above us. A door opened in the bottom of the ship. A bright light was shining down.

"I guess this is good-bye, Space Rock," I said. "I'm sorry I was angry."

"Forget it, Bob," he said. "You saved me!"

Space Rock floated up in the light.

But he did not go into the ship. He
floated under the opening and made
strange sounds.

Then four other rocks floated down.

They all began to sing. No one had
ever heard music like this before. It
sounded like the wind between the stars.
It sounded like the fire of the sun.

It was <u>real</u> rock music.

The kids had all gathered around. When the song was over they clapped and clapped. Miss Goodheart stood with her hands on her heart.

Space Rock and his friends floated up into the ship.

"Good-bye, Space Rock!" everyone yelled.

The ship went straight up, past the clouds.

Then it was gone.

"Wow!" said the kids.

"Wow!" said Miss Goodheart. "That was the <u>ultimate</u> show and tell!"

I never felt happier in my life.

A week later one of the balloon post cards came in the mail. We had written PLEASE WRITE DATE AND PLACE FOUND AND DROP IN MAILBOX.

This one was addressed to me. It said: FOUND APRIL 29 INSIDE SPACESHIP UNAR. NOW BOUND FOR HOME. GOOD-BYE, BOB— UNTIL WE MEET AGAIN—SPACE ROCK.